11/06

D1543687

MIDLOTHIAN
PUBLIC LIBRARY

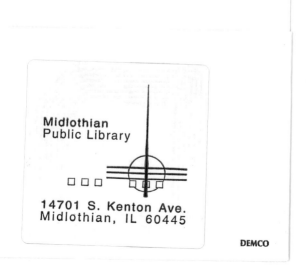

Famous Places of the World

of the World

Asia

Helen Bateman and Jayne Denshire

Smart Apple Media

This edition first published in 2006 in the United States of America by Smart Apple Media.

Smart Apple Media
2140 Howard Drive West
North Mankato
Minnesota 56003

First published in 2006 by
MACMILLAN EDUCATION AUSTRALIA PTY LTD
627 Chapel Street, South Yarra, Australia 3141

Visit our Web site at www.macmillan.com.au

Associated companies and representatives throughout the world.

Library of Congress Cataloging-in-Publication Data

Bateman, Helen.
  Asia / by Helen Bateman and Jayne Denshire.
    p. cm. — (Famous places of the world)
  Includes index.
  ISBN-13: 978-1-58340-800-1 (alk. paper)
  1. Asia—Description and travel—Juvenile literature. 2. Historic sites—Asia—Juvenile literature.
  I. Denshire, Jayne. II. Title.

  DS10.B28 2006
  950—dc22   2006002520

Project management by Limelight Press Pty Ltd
Design by Stan Lamond, Lamond Art & Design
Illustrations by Marjorie Crosby-Fairall
Maps by Lamond Art & Design and Andrew Davies
Map icons by Andrew Davies
Research by Kathy Gerrard
Consultant: Colin Sale BA (Sydney) MSc (London)

Printed in the United States

Acknowledgments
The authors and the publisher are grateful to the following for permission to reproduce
copyright material:

Cover photograph: Great Wall of China, courtesy of Dallas Heaton/Photolibrary.com
Atlas Picture Library/Colin Sale p. 24; APL/Corbis/Roger Wood p. 20; Getty Images/Bobby Model
p. 11 (top); Getty Images/Hugh Sitton p. 17; Getty Images/Luca Tettoni p. 18, Getty images/Juliet
Coombe p. 19; Getty Images/Robert Harding p. 26; iStockphoto/Wang Sanjun p. 4 (left); iStockphoto/
Sue Colvil p. 4 (centre left); iStockphoto/Christine Gonsalves p. 4. (centre right); iStockphoto/Wang
Sanjun p. 4 (right); iStockphoto/Aravind Teki p. 6; iStockphoto/Wang Sanjun p. 9; iStockphoto/Wang
Sanjun p. 10; iStockphoto/Wang Sanjun p. 11 (bottom); iStockphoto/Said Erdogan p. 25 (bottom);
iStockphoto/Israel Talby p. 29 (bottom); Lonely Planet/Dallas Stribley p.7; Lonely Planet/Keren Su p. 8;
Lonely Planet/Tom Cockrem p. 13 (top); Lonely Planet/Juliet Coombe p. 13 (bottom); Lonely Planet/
Glenn Beanland p. 14; Lonely Planet/John Elk III p. 16; Lonely Planet/John Borthwick p. 21; Lonely
Planet/Bob Charlton p. 22; Lonely Planet/Martin Moos p. 25 (top); Lonely Planet/Patrick Horton p. 27;
Seiden Allan/Photolibrary.com p. 23.

Contents

When a word in the text is printed in **bold**. You can look up its meaning in the Glossary on page 31.

Wonders of Asia

Asia is the world's biggest **continent** and comprises one-third of the Earth's land. Several religions and cultures have evolved there. There are many famous places in Asia. Some are ancient and some are modern. In Asia, most famous places have been built by humans, but there are also many natural wonders.

What makes a place famous?

The most common reasons why places become famous are because of their:

- **formation** how they were formed by nature
- **construction** how they were built by humans
- **antiquity** their age, dating back to ancient times
- **size** their height, width, length, volume, or area
- **function** how they work, or what they are used for
- **cultural importance** their value to the customs and society of the country
- **religious importance** their value to the religious beliefs of the country

ZOOM IN
The world's five major religions, Judaism, Christianity, Islam, Buddhism, and Hinduism all began in Asia.

Famous places in Asia

Asia has many famous places. Some are built structures and some are features created by nature.

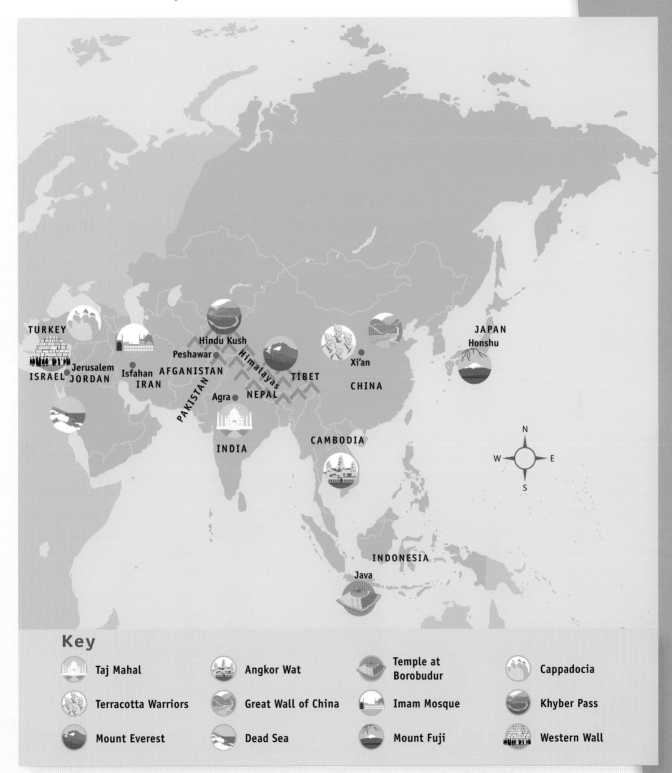

Key

- Taj Mahal
- Terracotta Warriors
- Mount Everest
- Angkor Wat
- Great Wall of China
- Dead Sea
- Temple at Borobudur
- Imam Mosque
- Mount Fuji
- Cappadocia
- Khyber Pass
- Western Wall

Taj Mahal

FACT FINDER

Location **Agra, India**

Date built **1631–1653**

Height **200 feet (60 m)**

WORLD HERITAGE SITE
since 1983

The Taj Mahal is a built structure that is famous for its construction and cultural importance. It was built by Shah Jahan, the **Mogul** emperor of India in the 1600s, as a **tomb** for his wife, Mumtaz Mahal. She died giving birth to their 14th child. This huge marble **mausoleum** is on the banks of the sacred Yamuna River, near Agra.

▼ The Taj Mahal stands on a red sandstone platform in a rectangular garden. A long channel of water lined with trees leads up to the gate of the tomb.

► The interior of the Taj Mahal is decorated with precious stones and raised carvings.

Framed by towers

The building sits on a huge platform with a **minaret**, or tower, at each corner. The building is made from brick and rubble, and is covered with white marble that is held in place with metal rods. In the central chamber, or room, lies a memorial slab to Mumtaz Mahal. The slab is covered with precious stones laid out to form flowers and decorative shapes.

Rulers of a Muslim empire

The Moguls were a Muslim empire that ruled India from the 1500s to the 1800s. In that time, many emperors ruled the land and Shah Jahan was the fifth of these rulers. He was interested in architecture and developed new techniques for finishing buildings. He used precious materials to build with, such as marble, instead of red sandstone. The Taj Mahal is known throughout the world for its unique shape and beautiful decoration.

► The main dome of the Taj Mahal is actually two domes, one inside the other. By having two domes, the structure is better supported on the soft sands of the riverbank on which it is situated.

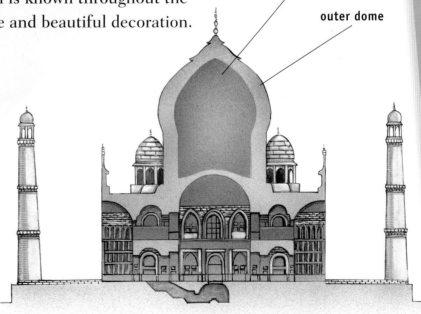

inner dome

outer dome

Terracotta Warriors

The terracotta warriors are built structures that are famous for their construction and cultural importance. Thousands of soldier statues were buried more than 2,000 years ago to protect the tomb of Emperor Qin Shi Huang Di. As recently as 1974, local farmers discovered the army of figures when they were digging a well.

A clay army

Among the army are foot soldiers, archers, commanders, soldiers on horseback and in chariots, all made from baked terracotta clay. The figures have hollow heads and bodies, and solid legs, all of which were made separately then put together with strips of clay. Each figure was then covered with a layer of fine clay, and its facial and clothing details were carved out before being baked hard.

ZOOM IN

Thousands of metal weapons have been unearthed near the warriors. They are still sharp today, probably as sharp as when they were buried 2,000 years ago.

◄ Facial and head features as well as clothing details were carved out of a fine layer of clay that covered each figure.

Learning about life

The details and layout of the terracotta warriors tell us a lot about life in China at the time of the Qin **dynasty**. They show how skilled the clay sculptors were. They also mark an important change in the way people were buried in China at that time. **Archeologists** have worked out that when the pits were first built, they were covered with timber beams with straw and bamboo mats between. The beams have left dents at the top of the walls of the pits.

The unearthing of the terracotta warriors is one of the most notable archeological discoveries in the world.

▲ The warriors have been discovered in rows in four separate pits. In the first and second pits almost 7,500 figures were found. The third pit had fewer figures, probably all commanders. The fourth pit was empty.

ZOOM IN
The figures were once painted with bright colors, but they have faded with time.

Mount Everest

FACT FINDER

Location **Himalayas, Tibet and Nepal**

Height **29,035 feet (8,850 m)**

Mount Everest is a natural landform that is famous for its size and religious importance. It is the world's highest mountain and the main mountain of the Himalayas, a mountain range that runs through central Asia. Buddhists believe that the Tibetan goddess Miyolangsangma lives on Mount Everest.

ZOOM IN
Buddhists believe that the peak of the mountain symbolizes a form of life that exists outside life on Earth.

▼ Wind, snow, and ice have shaped the sharp peaks and ridges of Mount Everest and the Himalayas over millions of years.

◄ This climber is heading down the Khumbu ice fall, the most dangerous part of the southern route on Mount Everest.

A challenging climb

The size of Mount Everest makes it a very difficult mountain to climb. Still, over 25,000 people a year reach the camps at the mountain's base. Strong winds and sudden **avalanches** create great danger for climbers.

Sherpas, who come from Nepal, take **expeditions** to the base camp. They carry everything the climbers need. The sherpas try to behave well on the mountain and seek blessings from monks so they do not offend the mountain goddess.

A mountainous barrier

Because Mount Everest and the Himalayas are so high, they stop warm, moist air from reaching Tibet and China. The air gets blocked by the mountain and cools, which turns the moisture to falling snow. This sacred mountain is known the world over for its massive size.

INSIDE STORY

Edmund Hillary and his sherpa, Tenzing Norgay, were the first team to climb Mount Everest. But the climb was not easy. One of the biggest problems to overcome was climbing high up where there is little oxygen. In 1953, using oxygen equipment, they took three hours to climb from the base camp of the mountain to the top. After their arrival, they hugged each other as a sign of their friendship then turned off their oxygen to hear the peaceful silence.

▲ Sherpas string up prayer flags to keep the mountain goddess happy before they head up the mountain.

Angkor Wat

ZOOM IN
Angkor Wat is a symbolic representation of the Hindu universe in its plan and layout.

FACT FINDER

Location **Cambodia**

Date built **1113–1150**

Area of temple site **21 hectares (52 ac)**

WORLD HERITAGE SITE since 1992

Angkor Wat is a built structure that is famous for its construction and religious importance. This temple is one of the temples from the ancient city of Angkor. It is the largest religious monument ever constructed, and holds special significance for followers of the Hindu faith.

▼ Most of the temple is made from sandstone and a harder volcanic stone. Parts of the stone were carved to look like timber and bamboo.

◄ The gallery walls on the second terrace are decorated with raised stone carvings of Hindu dancers, called Apsaras.

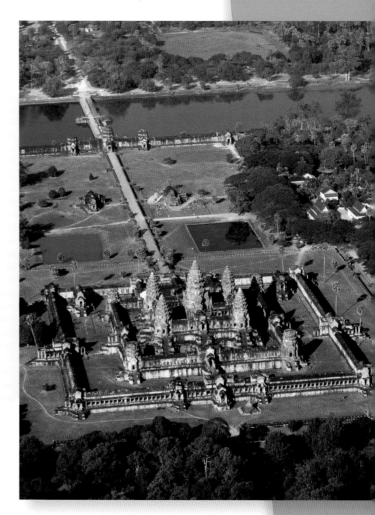

Surrounded by water

The temple **complex** is built on a rectangular island that is surrounded by a **moat**. A 820-foot (250-m) -long **causeway** leads from the moat to the main temple. This temple was built by a ruler called Suryavarman II to honour the Hindu god, Vishnu. It is more a **shrine** for Vishnu than a place of worship.

A three-layered pyramid

The temple is a pyramid with three **terraces**, one on top of each other. The bottom terrace is enclosed by a gallery with carvings of stories from Hindu holy books on its walls. The second terrace was used by priests. The third terrace is reached by 12 staircases and has five towers. Vishnu is said to live in the largest of the towers.

Today, Angkor Wat is still a functioning temple and is looked after by **UNESCO**, Japan, and France.

▲ The causeway that leads to the temple runs through a gate with three towers, past two pavilions and two pools into a central court.

ZOOM IN
Many local people thought that the monuments at Angkor Wat had been built by the gods.

Great Wall of China

The Great Wall of China is a built structure that is famous for its construction, size, and antiquity. The wall consists of several sections built over hundreds of years. It covers rugged **terrain** and goes through many environments. Some parts are quite flat, but others are much steeper.

The Great Wall was built to keep invaders to the north of China, known as Huns, out of Chinese lands.

▼ The Great Wall was built from earth and stone. Some of the sections were covered in bricks.

► During the most recent periods of building in the 1300s, forts were constructed along the way which held large numbers of troops.

A variety of materials

The building materials for the Great Wall varied depending on what was available in each region. In the west it was made from rammed earth and some parts were covered in sun-dried bricks. In the east, stone and fired bricks were used.

Keeping watch

Thousands of forts and watchtowers were built along the way so that soldiers could keep watch for the enemy. Messages were passed from tower to tower using smoke, drums, and cannons to signal danger. Extra paths and loops were constructed to confuse the invaders. Sometimes as many as 20 different routes of the wall made it difficult for the invaders to know which way to go.

The Great Wall is known throughout the world as a built structure that blends beautifully with its natural surroundings.

fort

Dead Sea

ZOOM IN
The Dead Sea is nine times as salty as the ocean.

FACT FINDER

Location border of Jordan and Israel

Length 31 miles (50 km)

Width up to 17 miles (28 km)

Depth up to 1,300 feet (400 m)

Date first formed 23 million years ago

The Dead Sea is a natural feature that is famous for its formation, function, and religious importance. This salty lake lies at the lowest point of dry land on Earth. It was given its name because nothing can live in its highly salty waters. The water is some of the saltiest in the world.

The oldest biblical documents ever found were discovered on the lake's northern shores.

Salty water everywhere

The water in the Dead Sea contains lots of minerals, mainly composed of salt. These minerals make up about one-third of the water's content. The high level of salt makes floating easy and the salty water is said to have healing powers.

The climate of the Dead Sea region is very hot and dry, so the water **evaporates** easily. When the water evaporates, large amounts of salt are left behind that build up along the shoreline.

◄ The mineral salt that collects at the water's edge is processed on the lake's shores for table salt, medicine, and fertilizers.

A place of history

The Dead Sea is associated with various historic and religious events. Traces of Greek, Roman, Christian, Muslim, and Jewish life are found in the area. The biblical sites of Sodom and Gomorrah are thought to be submerged under the Dead Sea. It was one of the first health retreats for Herod the Great and where he built many **fortresses**. It supplied **embalming** materials for **mummies** in ancient Egyptian times.

Many animals are able to live in the mountains surrounding the Dead Sea. Foxes, hares, camels, and even leopards roam this dry, hilly terrain. The Dead Sea is famous for its low location, salty water, and memorable historic events.

▲ It is impossible to sink in the Dead Sea because the extremely salty water keeps you constantly afloat.

ZOOM IN
The Dead Sea is also known as the Sea of Lot. In the Bible, God was said to have turned Lot's wife into the pillar of salt that stands on one corner of the lake.

INSIDE STORY
The Dead Sea Scrolls are documents from biblical times. The first scrolls were discovered in 1947 by a young boy who was looking for his lost goat. He came across some caves at Qumran on the Dead Sea. Inside the caves were hundreds of documents sealed inside pottery jars. The dry air of the Dead Sea had stopped the documents from wearing away. People learned more about biblical times from the discovery of these documents.

Temple at Borobudur

The Temple at Borobudur is a built structure that is famous for its construction and religious importance. This temple is a **stupa**, or pyramid, built to honour Buddha, the god of the local people. It was constructed to remind the people of their Buddhist beliefs. There are galleries on the lower levels of the temple with carvings and sculptures that show aspects of religious life.

▼ The temple sits on a large base. It has five square, terraced levels, then three circular terraces with a massive stupa on top.

► On the circular levels, a Buddha sits inside each stupa. Some of the Buddhas, like this one, have lost the outer shell of their stupa.

ZOOM IN

Around 1.6 million andesite stones were used in the temple.

Sitting on stone

This temple is built over a **hillock** on a base made from volcanic stone called andesite. The base once had many sculptures around its rim but most of these have now gone. Five terraced levels rise up from the base. These levels have almost 3 miles (5 km) of walkways with over 500 Buddhas.

On the three circular levels are over 70 bell-shaped stupas covered in bricks. The brickwork has been laid out with spaces between each brick.

Life on the walls

Carved panels on the square levels show scenes from everyday life in the 800s, such as elephants, dancing girls, warriors, and kings. The circular levels have special spiritual meaning.

Parts of this famous temple were rebuilt between 1973 and 1984 to better preserve it. Some of the temple was destroyed in 1985, but it has been totally restored by UNESCO in recent times.

ZOOM IN

It was thought to be good luck to reach through the holes of the smaller stupas and touch the Buddhas inside.

19

Imam Mosque

FACT FINDER

Location **Isfahan, Iran**

Date built **1611–1629**

Height **167 feet (51 m)**

WORLD HERITAGE SITE
since 1979

The Imam Mosque is a built structure that is famous for its construction and religious importance. The mosque was built as part of Isfahan, Persia's new capital city in the early 1600s. Persia, now Iran, had been won back from the fierce Ottoman empire and the creation of Isfahan symbolised the start of a new era.

ZOOM IN
The mosque is positioned so that it faces the religious city of Mecca, like all mosques.

▼ The mosque sits at one end of Imam Square. There are two minarets, or towers, at the mosque's entrance gate and two on the mosque itself.

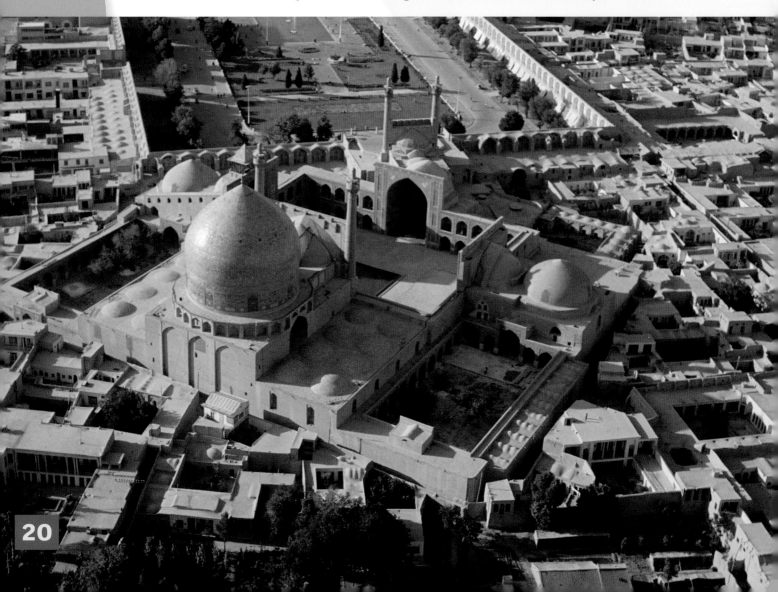

A place to pray

The mosque has an entrance corridor from the city square, a courtyard, and quiet spots for meditation and prayer. Religious teachers give their teachings in two school rooms, or madraseh. The main dome of the mosque is hollow, with an inner ceiling then the outer roof. The inside and outside of the building are decorated with **mosaics** made from majolica tiles. These tiles are ceramic and are painted with blue, white and gold enamel.

The religious role

The Imam Mosque holds great religious significance for Muslims. Quotations from the Koran, the holy book of Islam, are created in the tile work. The names of Mohammed and Ali, the Muslim prophets, are written in beautiful script on the walls. The detailed decoration and construction of the Imam Mosque make it a world-famous structure.

▲ Almost every surface of the mosque is covered with majolica tiles laid out in geometric, religious, and floral designs.

ZOOM IN
Over 18 million bricks and 470,000 tiles cover the surface of the mosque.

Mount Fuji

ZOOM IN
Women have only been allowed to climb Mount Fuji since the late 1800s.

FACT FINDER

Location Honshu, Japan

Height 12,388 feet (3,776 m)

Distance around base 78 miles (125 km)

Mount Fuji is a natural landform that is famous for its formation, size, and cultural importance. It is Japan's highest mountain. Mount Fuji is still considered to be an **active volcano**, although it has not erupted for about 300 years. It holds special significance for followers of the Shinto religion in Japan.

▼ Mount Fuji is important to followers of the Shinto religion, especially when the cherry blossoms bloom in Spring.

► Each year thousands of religious followers, or pilgrims, climb Mount Fuji in their traditional clothes. They reach the top by sunrise, a time when the mountain has a pink tinge.

Four volcanoes in one

The cone shape of Mount Fuji was created from not one, but four volcanoes that have **evolved** over time. The current Mount Fuji is the youngest. It has existed for the past 100,000 years. Each time it erupted during that time, volcanic **lava** covered the other older mountains, which now lie underneath.

ZOOM IN
Mount Fuji has erupted 100 times in the last 10,000 years.

A sacred place

Mount Fuji has been worshipped in Japan since ancient times. It is considered to be sacred and has temples and shrines on and near it. Many people in Japan follow the Shinto religion and worship the beauty of nature. So the changing sights of Mount Fuji at different times hold great value. The religious meaning and perfect cone shape of Mount Fuji make it Japan's most symbolic natural wonder.

► Over time, four volcanoes have erupted to help give Mount Fuji its current shape. Ko-Mitake and Ashitakayama erupted in the same period and are the oldest. Ko-Fuji formed the base of Shin-Fuji, the current Mount Fuji.

MOUNT FUJI'S FORMATION

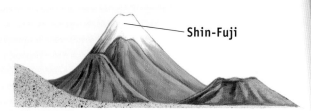

Shin-Fuji

10 thousand years ago

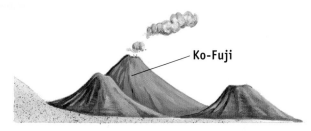

Ko-Fuji

15 thousand years ago

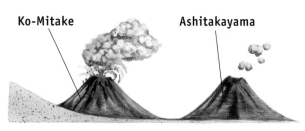

Ko-Mitake   Ashitakayama

200 thousand years ago

Cappadocia

ZOOM IN

The cone-shaped formations at Cappadocia are often called fairy chimneys, or "kalelar" meaning "castles," by the locals.

FACT FINDER

Location eastern central Turkey

Date created 2500 B.C. to present

WORLD HERITAGE SITE
  since 1985

Cappadocia is a natural region that is famous for its formation. Built structures also form part of its unique appearance. Unusual cone-shaped formations appear across the landscape. Many cities have been carved out of soft rock, in the cones and under the ground.

Fairy chimney landscape

The fairy chimney formations that appear above the ground and the dwellings under the ground have been built from a soft volcanic stone called tuff. The tuff was created millions of years ago from **volcanic ash** that exploded out of three volcanoes in the area and fell from the sky. Over time, running water eroded the tuff to form valleys and the fairy chimneys that now dot the landscape. Some stacks have chunks of harder rock balancing on top that look like hats.

▼ The formations at Cappadocia are a variety of shapes, from columns and pyramids to twisted cones and needles.

◄ Tunnels were built to link the various settlements under the ground.

Life underground

More than 30 underground cities have been found by archeologists. Inside the houses in these settlements are chairs, tables, and beds all carved out of tuff stone. Some settlements also have churches with painted **frescoes** on the walls. At the town of Nevsehir is a cave that leads to an underground settlement with eight different levels.

Cappadocia combines unusual natural landforms and built structures in one of the world's most famous wonders.

INSIDE STORY

Throughout history, the region where Cappadocia is situated was often invaded. During these times, the locals used the underground dwellings to hide from the enemy. Once they were underground, they would roll heavy stones in front of the entrance for protection. The locals would sometimes stay there for months with the enemy above unaware they were under them.

▲ Sometimes a chunk of harder rock protects the underlying layer of soft rock from eroding. So the hard rock is left balancing on top of the tall, soft formation.

Khyber Pass

ZOOM IN

For hundreds of years, camel processions, known as caravans, traveled through the Khyber Pass bringing goods to trade.

FACT FINDER

Location Afghanistan and Pakistan

Length 33 miles (53 km)

Highest point 3,510 feet (1,070 m)

Narrowest point 10 feet (3 m)

The Khyber Pass is a built structure that is famous for its construction. It is the most important pass, or mountain route, connecting Pakistan and Afghanistan. It has also played an important, although violent, part in history during times of war and conflict between countries and cultures in this region of Asia.

▼ The Khyber Pass starts near the town of Peshawar in Pakistan, then weaves its way through the mountains to near the border of Afghanistan.

► The railway through the Khyber Pass opened in 1925. If the area gets too dangerous, the train does not run.

ZOOM IN
Some parts of the pass are so steep that two steam engines are needed to pull and push just a few carriages.

A winding mountain route

This part of Asia is mountainous with some desert. The Khyber Pass is a winding route 33 miles (53 km) long that cuts through a part of the Hindu Kush mountain range. It creates the most direct land route between India and Pakistan. There is a sealed road through the pass as well as a railway. Tribes live in the surrounding area and use their laws to rule the region.

Traders and travellers

The Khyber Pass has been a vital route for armies, traders and peaceful travelers for hundreds of years. The Moguls, a fierce group from the north of Asia, used the pass in the 1300s to invade the south. Later, in the 1800s and 1900s, British troops from India used the pass to travel north and gain control over Afghanistan.

The Khyber Pass is best known as a travel route and for its role in wars and **conflict**.

INSIDE STORY

The region around the Khyber Pass was controlled by the British in the late 1800s. During that time, some local tribesmen formed a military group connected to the British troops, known as the Khyber Rifles, who helped to keep order in the region. They fought on Britain's side in World War II. When Pakistan gained independence in 1947, these men took on new duties, such as protecting the border from terrorists.

Western Wall

FACT FINDER

Location **Jerusalem, Israel**

Date built **20 B.C.**

Length **161 feet (49 m)**

Height **69 feet (21 m)**

The Western Wall is a built structure that is famous for its religious importance and construction. It is in the Old City of Jerusalem. It is the holiest of holy places for people of the Jewish faith around the world. King Herod built this wall when he extended the Temple Mount, which was set into the side of a mountain. In 70 A.D. the Romans destroyed Herod's temple and the Jews were forced out of Jerusalem. The remains of the wall became an important symbol for Jews.

ZOOM IN
The Temple Mount on which the wall stands is holy to both Jews and Muslims.

▼ Near the Western Wall stands the Dome of the Rock, which is Jerusalem's holiest Islamic place.

▶ When Jews come to the wall to pray, they face the wall and touch the blocks while they say their prayers.

◀ Visitors to the wall write special prayers on pieces of paper and push them into the cracks between the blocks.

Building blocks

The wall is built from large limestone blocks. The size of the blocks varies but the largest is 7.7 feet (5.4 m) long. The stones do not have **mortar** between them because they are so closely fitted together. Repairs have been done to the wall since it was first built and new, smaller stones have been added.

Western or Wailing Wall

The Western Wall was also known as the Wailing Wall. Jews would return to the wall to tear their clothes and wail, or cry. This was done as a symbol of what Jewish people had lost in Jerusalem and the destruction of Herod's temple. Now thousands of Jews from all over the world visit the wall each year to touch it and to pray. The wall is like an outdoor synagogue, or church, with separate sections for men and for women. Today this world-famous monument is seen as a place to celebrate the coming together of Jews.

ZOOM IN
Today Jews commonly call this sacred site simply "The Wall" as everyone knows which wall they are talking about.

Famous places of Asia

Our world has a rich collection of famous places. Some are spectacular natural wonders and some are engineering or architectural masterpieces. These famous places in Asia are outstanding in many different ways.

Wonders formed by nature

PLACE	FAMOUS FOR
Mount Everest	The tallest mountain in the world
Dead Sea	Occurs at the lowest land level on Earth Some of the saltiest water in the world
Mount Fuji	The tallest mountain in Japan Sacred to followers of the Shinto religion
Cappadocia	A region with unusual rock formations and ancient underground dwellings

Masterpieces built by humans

PLACE	FAMOUS FOR
Taj Mahal	One of the most elaborately decorated buildings in the world
Terracotta Warriors	The largest collection of statues discovered in modern times
Angkor Wat	The largest religious monument ever constructed
Great Wall of China	The longest wall ever constructed A perfect blend of built and natural elements
Temple of Borobudur	One of the most important Buddhist temples in the world
Imam Mosque	It was built as the central building in Isfahan, the capital of Persia, now Iran
Khyber Pass	The most direct route between Afghanistan and Pakistan
Western Wall	The holiest of holy places for Jews

Glossary

active volcano a volcano that is able to erupt at any time

archeologists people who study the people and customs of ancient times from the buildings they left behind

avalanches large masses of ice or snow that slide suddenly down a mountain slope

causeway a raised road across wet ground or water

complex a group of buildings

conflict fighting or disagreement

continent one of the main land masses of the world

dynasty a series of rulers who belong to the same family

embalming treating a dead body with chemicals to preserve it

evaporates takes moisture out of something so that it dries up

evolved developed gradually to become something else

expeditions travel goups

fortresses forts built to protect from the enemy

frescoes paintings done on a plastered wall or ceiling

hillock a mound of earth

lava hot liquid rock that comes from a volcano

mausoleum a grand tomb

minaret a tall tower built on or next to a Muslim mosque, from which an official calls the people to prayer

moat a deep, wide ditch, usually filled with water, surrounding a town or building to help keep invaders out

Mogul a group who ruled northern Asia in the 1600s

mortar a mixture used for joining bricks together

mosaics pictures made by joining together small pieces of stone, glass, or tiling

mummies dead bodies that have been specially treated to stop them from decaying

Sherpas a special group of people from Tibet, near the Himalaya mountains

shrine a sacred or holy place

stupa a cone- or dome-shaped monument in memory of Buddha

terrain a part of the land surface

terraces raised levels of a building

tomb a grave, especially for important people

UNESCO stands for United Nations Educational, Scientific, and Cultural Organization. An agency of the United Nations that helps with educational and cultural programs.

volcanic ash tiny particles of solid lava that fall from the sky after a volcanic explosion

Index